This is My Story
for the
Glory of God

Jerry Lee Schock

This is My Story for the Glory of God

Copyright © 2023 by Jerry Lee Schock

Paperback ISBN: 978-1-63812-715-4
Ebook ISBN: 978-1-63812-714-7

All rights reserved. No part in this book may be produced and transmitted in any form or by any means, electronic, or mechanical, including photocopying, recording, or by any information storage and retrieval system, without permission in writing from the copyright owner.

The views expressed in this work are solely those of the author and do not necessarily reflect the views of the publisher. It hereby disclaims any responsibility for them.

Published by Pen Culture Solutions   05/04/2023

Pen Culture Solutions
1-888-727-7204 (USA)
1-800-950-458 (Australia)
support@penculturesolutions.com

This is My Story

for the

Glory of God

Preface

For years I have watched people trust a savior they have never seen to take them to heaven they have never seen but yet they cannot trust him to handle their everyday problems, God has promised, he will never leave us, nor forsake us, and that is a promise that will last forever. God has carried me through many things in my life, devastating things, the loss of a child. Something I never dreamed of, and yet he has carried me, taken care of me, and given me a continuing faith that will not waiver about His ability to take care of me. I would encourage those who have problems with faith to remember the words that I was given by my Bible club teacher before I spoke on faith my senior year in high school forsaking all I take him, and that truly is what faith is made of force taking everything else, and leaving it behind, and accepting the Lord Jesus, to take care of us with our everyday issues, we truly must trust him we must trust the fact that God allowed his only son to die on Calvary for our sins and that gave us a promise of heaven. Once we go home to meet the Lord, hold that faith close to your heart and trust in the Lord for everything there's not one need that you will ever have in this life that God will not meet sometimes it's not in the way you expect, but it's always the way it should be His will is best for our lives. We need to seek God's will in all things, knowing that He always knows what's best for us. God sees a lot farther down the road than we can. He knows every rock and stony place that our feet will ever touch in this life and remember he has walked that road ahead of you you'll never walk into a valley where you're walking alone God always took those steps ahead and prepare the way for whatever we're asked to go through in this life, trust in him believe in him allow him to control your future and you will never go wrong. With love and prayers Jerry Lee as I write "My Story for God's Glory."

I was born Jerry Lee Schock on March 25, 1943, to Ada Lee and Jeremiah Schock. Sixteen months later, my first brother Stanley Thomas was born and, four and a half years later, my youngest brother Jeremiah Jr.

My father was an alcoholic and abuser, and eventually, Mom ended up divorcing him. Mom said he would start drinking on Friday and stay drunk until Monday morning time to go to work. But he never missed a day of work due to alcoholism. My father was a very intelligent man according to my mother, as he was the head of industrial planning for years at Wright Patterson Air Force Base in Dayton, Ohio. Mother always said we had Dad's brain whenever we excelled in whatever we were doing.

Our mother was born Ada Lee Herman to Frank and Mabel Herman on May 10, 1921, in Miamisburg, Ohio.

My grandfather, Frank W. Herman, died at the age of ninety-seven at home and had been in ill health so that Grandma had to feed him and bathe him in bed. Grandma was a small woman, not very tall at all, and Grandpa was over six feet tall, so it made it a little bit hard on her, but she continued to take care of him for years I can remember feeding Grandpa when we were living there before Mom and Dad divorced. We were there for some period of time, and every Saturday morning without fail, when he was able, since I was his favorite, Grandpa and I would walk to Andy's market going down the alley through Miamisburg, and he would always buy me a candy bar. All of the grandchildren got $1 in their birthday cards, but Grandpa always put an extra one in for me.

He had a parakeet named Petey, and when we were watching the Cincinnati Reds play baseball, Petey would come out of his cage and sit on Grandpa's head while we watched the baseball game. I would be at Grandpa's feet, and he was in his easy chair. Some precious memories there of time we spent together.

Grandma died at Miami Valley Hospital on New Year's Eve at the age of seventy-six, the year Grandpa died not lasting long after my grandpa had gone.

Mabel Herman, my grandmother, was born on a boat in neutral water coming over from Germany and considered to be a woman without a country.

Mother graduated high school from Miamisburg then married our dad, Jeremiah Schock. She died at ninety years of age. I called Mom the year she turned ninety on May 10 to wish her a happy birthday and asked what she was doing. My brother Stan was there. They had come for her birthday, and she said he was dressing her arm because she had fallen against the bathtub. For several months, I had tried to get her an emergency button in case of a fall. She refused until that day when I asked, she finally said yes. I ordered the button, and it was delivered with my younger brother Jerry, making sure everything was hooked up properly and working.

Mom had a brain bleed, the first part of July 2011. She pushed her emergency button and fell in the kitchen, striking her head on the counter. The paramedics took a window out on the front porch to get in and take her to the hospital. I spoke to the doctor on the phone, and he asked about her wishes for life support. I told him Mom did not want life support. The doctor said if they were to drill into her brain to try to relieve the bleeding, she would probably be in intensive care unresponsive; and it could be, he said, for months at her age with the health she was in. So no life support or anything extra was done as Mother requested it not be. She chose to just go naturally when it came time to die. She stayed at Miami Valley Hospital for just a short time and then was put into hospice. Stan, Phyllis, Jerry, and I were all there with her, and I remember the nurse telling us, as Mom lingered, she had some unfinished business. I quickly explained to her that Mom never left things undone. She followed through on what she always told us kids—if you have something you want to do, you better do it today because tomorrow may not come.

I remember on a Saturday asking her if I could go home the next day (no one else knew how to do the payroll), and she said yes. Stan spoke up and said she means Georgia and Mom immediately came back with "I know where she lives" very emphatically. She was very alert and very aware of what was going on around her—thank the Lord—until the very end.

She died on July 19, 2011, about 4:30 a.m. after about two weeks in hospice.

Her brother Bill died at the age of eighty-four on January 2010. Aunt Mary Schröder, her sister, died at the age of ninety-seven on August 15, 2011. They never knew her mother was in hospice or the hospital.

I still miss talking to Mom so much today.

She was always so encouraging. I regret she didn't live long enough to know God allowed me to publish the poetry, but she would have been proud. I know she would've said, "See, honey, that angel is still on your shoulder," as I heard her say so many times in my life. She was a very special woman, and the love she had for her children was extremely evident. It was not always easy for her, but she always saw that we had what we needed. There certainly was not a lot of excess, but it was never a lack of love. She worked hard to take care of us, and I will be forever grateful for the faith she showed and taught us.

Bobby Joe, my son, was born on November 14, 1962, and died in a motorcycle wreck on May 21, 1986, as I said earlier. Jeanne, who had been Dad's secretary at Wright Patterson Air Force Base, my precious stepmother and I used to go bowling with the kids and spend time together. She was at the house after Bobby Joe died and asked if I had a gravesite for him, and I told her no. She gave me the grave next to my father to bury my son. I will never forget that kindness. Even after Dad died, she and Tammy, my half-sister, and I stayed in touch. We went bowling together, and we are in touch today on Facebook. Such a precious friend.

* * *

I remember when I was thirteen years old sitting in our living room, and Mother told me that I always had an angel on my shoulder, and she had watched him work things out for me that would never work out for anyone else. It has only been recently that I realized what a blessing she pronounced on my life. My brothers and I walked to the City Mission every Sunday morning for church and Sunday school.

Hobart Roark preached and taught Sunday school and his wife, Thelma, played the piano. They owned a furniture store and fur shop in Laura, Ohio. Thelma took a liking to me, and on Friday would pick me up, and I would stay with them over the weekend through church on Sunday night. They attended Westwood Baptist Church in Dayton, Ohio, at the age of thirteen. I walked the aisle kneeling at the altar and invited Jesus into my heart. My life has never been the same.

Many times after Mom and Dad were divorced my grandmother would tell my mom, "You cannot raise those children alone."

Mom would say, "I am not raising them alone. God is with us." My grandmother insisted that Mother should not attempt that and put us in the children's home to which Mom replied she would work as many jobs as she needed to keep us together. At one time, she held three jobs. She worked at the restaurant, going to work very early in the morning to start the coffee urns. She called Bingo in the evening at the Pythian Castle and also had a newspaper branch for the *Dayton Daily News*. My father was from Mckee, Kentucky, and was extremely prejudiced against people of color. Mother would always say that the same God made us all and no matter what color a man's skin was if you cut him, we all bleed red. She taught us not to be prejudiced against anyone, for which I am so grateful. From grade school all the way to high school, my very best friend was a black girl named Virginia Glanton, but we lost touch after high school.

Mom stayed in food service. She worked at YMCA cafeteria as a cashier and took a liking to some of the exchange students from the Dominican Republic and invited them to our home. Since I was extremely interested in finding out if the people around me knew the Lord, I invited Ramon Diaz to go to church with me, and we got on the bus on a Sunday morning and went to church. The minute that we walked into the church, I can still remember the coldness because Ramon was from another country and his skin was dark. I could feel the chill as if someone had poured a tray of ice over the entire church as we walked down the aisle to go to sit in front of the church. I was very active in the church, in the choir, in Sunday school, and teaching junior church. I didn't realize that I was in Southern Baptist Church, and they were extremely prejudiced against people of color. I quickly learned about the word *prejudice* and *persecution* when several weeks later my Sunday school teacher took me home and told Mom to take me out of that church because I was being persecuted as I believed that everyone should be treated the same. This incident taught me two words I had never known, prejudice and persecution, leading me to my goal of becoming a missionary nurse and working in Africa.

Unlike today when I was in high school, we had a Bible club all four years, and I was blessed to be a part of it. We met once a week in the choir room. My senior year, our Bible club teacher asked if I would like to speak to our group. I told her yes, and she asked what I wanted to talk about. I said faith.

She said, "Let me give you something to help you," and wrote the word *faith* vertically by each letter and came up with this: "Forsaking all I take Him." That's something I have never forgotten, and it was such a blessing. God has continued to bless me my entire life although I have failed Him so many times.

When I got to high school, I signed up for chemistry and Latin to prepare for nursing school. After graduating high school in 1961 in the upper tenth of my graduating class at Stivers High School, I entered nurses training at Miami Valley Hospital to become an RN.

* * *

Mom told me growing up to stay chaste until marriage. Across the street from our apartment was a Texaco service station and I allowed a twenty-six-year-old man to take advantage of me. When he discovered I was pregnant, he tried everything to make me lose my baby. Once I knew I was pregnant, I called Mom from school and told her. The first words out of her mouth were, "Pack your clothes and come home." She told me we would raise my baby together and stayed true to her word. My son was born November 14, 1962, and I named him Bobby Joe.

Mother told me not to go after Bobby's daddy for support in order to keep him out of our lives, so I never did. He got married to an older woman the day before we were supposed to and left for Texas. Again, I could see God's hand of provision and protection.

Soon after Bobby was born, we moved into a house. Four years of junior achievement during high school prepared me for my first job at *Newsweek* magazine. Next door was a finance company. With an opportunity for more income, I applied for a job and was hired. Later taking a position with a construction company as a payroll clerk, I went to work for them closer to home. Across the street was a concrete company and one of the men, who was married, took an interest in me; and for some time, I stayed in a relationship I never should've been in out of God's will.

Eventually, Bobby Joe and I moved to West Carrollton, Ohio, into a two-room apartment. Next door was the West Carrollton Police Department. Around the corner was Robert's Furniture. When the bridge that was being built was finished, my payroll job ended. I walked into Robert's where I met Howard Smith known as Smitty. There were multiple buildings that made up the store on both sides of the street. I asked if they had any jobs; he wanted to know if I could sell. I told him I didn't know but was willing to try. The next customer in the door was mine. I greeted them. They were looking for a lamp for their commode, and it went through my mind we never put lamps on the commode at home, but

I asked them to show me what they liked and took them to the back room. They showed me their commode, which was an octagon-shaped table. I still laugh today about that. They picked out lamps.

As soon as I completed the sale, Smitty said anyone who can sell accessories can sell anything and I was hired. Thus began my career with Robert's Furniture. Smitty; Herb, Robert's owner; his brother, Leon; and myself were the sales staff. It was here I met Rudy and Juanita who came in looking for something in bedroom furniture, and over a period of time, we became great friends. Juanita's and my friendship lasted fifty years, and in that time, we never had an ill word for one another. She lived in Germantown, Ohio, and was not in the best of health. Her husband left her, and Rudy was a wonderful friend who continued to look after her. Juanita has since gone home to be with the Lord, but Rudy and I stayed in touch yet today.

*　*　*

Bobby and I moved into a two-bedroom apartment with the owner living on the other side. It was here I got my first car—a used 1965 Chevrolet convertible.

After a time, Herb filed for bankruptcy and moved back to Kentucky. I then went to work for a collection agency in Dayton.

Sometime later, I received a call from Ken Fletcher telling me he and Smitty were taking over the Roberts stores, and Smitty told him if they were to succeed, they needed me asking if I wanted to come to work and of course I did. Not being able to afford a sign, we changed the *T* to a *D* and became *Roberds*. Several years later moving into one building where everything was under one roof. Bobby and I then moved into an apartment on Alex Road and were attending Bible Baptist Church. At one point in time, I told the Lord I did not want to raise my son in an apartment, and when Bobby was around ten years old, the Lord permitted me to buy a home.

On Sunday night, the store was open until six and Bobby was around fourteen. I wound up going to church late one Sunday evening because of a late customer, but a youth director always picked him up for church on Sunday night. Because I was late coming in, I sat in the back of the church, which I never did. Bobby came up behind me very troubled at the age of fourteen telling me he didn't know what was wrong, but he was extremely troubled, so I took him out into the vestibule. I asked him if he really knew if he died today he'd go to heaven, and he told me no so I told him we had better make sure he knelt in the vestibule at the bench, asking the Lord Jesus into his heart, and we walked the aisle together and he was baptized that evening.

At some point, I was attending Moraine Heights Baptist Church. We had a nine-hundred-seat auditorium with Sunday school classes offices and the nursery around the perimeter of the auditorium. I was active in the choir doing solo work and worked as nursery coordinator. Smitty also attended there and was a deacon. At one point, the government said the church secretaries and those cleaning the churches had to be taxed and Social Security paid on them. Pastor Hudson said he refused to give God's money to Caesar, and since I was off Tuesday and Wednesday, I told him I would be happy to take over the secretarial duties at the church, which I did working with the bulletins and those printing them and the banking. Opening the desk, I found several years of bank statements that had never been reconciled, discovering our bank owed the church quite a sum of money. The copy machine really needed to be replaced, and Pastor said the money I had located that was owed to us paid for a new copier.

* * *

We opened our first satellite store in Piqua, Ohio. Over time, I had developed a list of things needed to open a new store with the satellite location in mind teaching myself how to use Lotus 1-2-3 and Word on the computer. The list became complete as I took it to others to add things not thought of and it became known as the shock list. I spent five years traveling for Roberds as corporate coordinator opening new stores. When they filed chapter 13 in December 2000, we had twenty-eight stores in four states including Ohio, Georgia, Florida, and Indiana.

Mother worked at the YMCA in the cafeteria during the day and cooked for a halfway home for ex-convicts where she met the man I married. To be honest, I told God what I wanted. I did not ask Him. Stepping out of God's will, we were married in Franklin, Ohio, and I knew the moment we got married it was a mistake. Jerry was an ex-convict who did time for writing bad checks.

He was very abusive and very unkind to my son although he never touched him, and had he done so, I would've divorced him much sooner than I did. We got into an argument, and he wound up beating my face into the floor and beating me up pretty badly. That was the last time he ever laid a hand on me. When I went to work the next day, I told them I had been in a car wreck, but Smitty looked at me and said he knew better telling me that my husband had beat me and if he ever showed his face at the store Smitty promised he would shoot him.

When the divorce was final, he never showed up in court; and my brother, who was a deputy for Montgomery County at the time, told him if he ever so much as drove down the street I lived on he would come after him. Since my ex-husband hated policemen, he never bothered me again. Thank the Lord. He ran around on me I guess the whole time we were married and was an attendant at a service station, and several times I would drive up and find a woman sitting on his lap; eventually, he told me his parole officer told him he needed to move back to Xenia, which was a lie and I found out several other lies were being told such as the fact that he was telling people he owned my home.

For two weeks before the divorce, Bobby and I had not been permitted to go home at my attorney's instructions, and I would go during the day and open the windows to air the house out as he had a Great Dane dog named Tigger, and it left odors in the house if the house was closed up. Jerry had taken the dog with him and left along with a small dog he had purchased for me for my birthday. Bobby and I went home after the divorce was final, and sitting on the couch, he became drowsy and said he smelled gas. So I called the Dayton power and light gas company, and when the man pulled up into the driveway, he was in a state of panic running asking me where the main gas line was and went into the utility room and found that Jerry had actually turned a fitting on the furnace, causing the pilot light to go out, and gas was leaking into the house. The man plainly said if anyone had lit a match, the house would have blown sky-high. I guess his last attempt was to try to kill us, but again the Lord protected us as promised.

I continued to travel opening stores. As I said, Mom was working at the YMCA as a cashier in the cafeteria, and she decided to retire at age sixty-five on May 10, 1986. On May 21, 1986, my son was killed in a motorcycle wreck. He had gotten out of God's will and was out drinking with his friends who tried desperately to put his motorcycle in their truck to bring him home. The boys told me later, and he refused to allow anyone to touch it. It was reported as he drove down Alex Road with a 45 mph speed limit doing at least 95 mph. He had no helmet on. To get to our home, you had to turn right at the railroad tracks where there was a curb before you cross them. He evidently realized he was going too fast. My brother later told me he must've put his cowboy boots down to brake and actually left the imprint of the boot's heel in the concrete at the curb missing the turn. His body was thrown into a parking lot across the railroad tracks where I was promised when I went home for his funeral and spoke to a sergeant at the police station. The moment the back of his head hit the pavement, he was gone. He always said if he put the cycle down for the last time, he wanted it to be fast. And God was good to us, he never suffered one bit and only was cut in the groin area where the cycle had come back on him, according to my brother when we went to the funeral home where I refused to see him, not wanting to remember him that way.

I was opening stores in Florida at the time, and my brother could not reach me as I was between stores on the road, so he called my boss, Ken, telling him what happened;

and Ken had my pastor, Travis Hudson, who called to the store in West Carrollton and called our office manager in Florida telling her when I came in not to let anyone talk to me but to take me to the president's office where my pastor would be calling me. It was amazing that he wanted my pastor called because he insisted I never talk about the Lord at work but leave it at home.

The company flew me home for Bobby's funeral with Bona, our designer, going with me on the plane. She later sent me a note when I returned to Tampa, thanking me for showing her what faith looked like during the time we traveled to go home and bury my child. Pastor Hudson came to the door when I reached home asking if I was okay, and I assured him I had known the Lord as my savior for a long time and the first thing I found out about God was He never made a mistake, and I knew He was not going to start with me. Again the promises of God were very prevalent in my life during that *VERY very* hard time.

My pastor, Travis Hudson, preached Bobby's funeral with a closed casket at my request again not wanting to remember him that way sent me a letter when I returned to Florida saying after nearly forty years of preaching, he had never seen what real faith looked like and thanked me for having seen it in me at the time of Bobby's funeral.

God has promised in his precious word never to leave us nor forsake us in Hebrews 13:5 and I can testify to that as many can. There's no way without the help of the Lord I could've gone through such a horrible time losing my only child. But again, I found God's grace to be sufficient and His protection to be there for me. At Bobby's funeral, Ken had asked Mom if she was going to move into my house, telling her I was traveling and no longer needed it. Mom was living in an apartment, and after Bobby's funeral since I was traveling, she moved into the house as I already had housing in Tampa due to multiple stores planned.

In 1987 after opening the next satellite store, I asked if I could move to Florida and was told I could. I got an apartment in St. Petersburg across the bridge from Tampa, which kept me close to several of our stores.

When I decided to move to Florida, the man I had been involved with for so many years decided he couldn't live without me and moved to Florida; but after one month, he missed his family so much. I went home from work one night and found a check on the counter for the next month's rent and a note that he missed his family too much and was going back home, probably without a doubt the best thing that God could have done for me. I got on the telephone the next day after getting the phone book out and started looking for churches knowing that I had to get my life right with the Lord or I was not going to be in this world much longer as God will not tolerate sin.

I found Bible Baptist Church in Pinellas Park and called to be sure what time they started, and that Sunday morning I showed up, went to the altar confessing my sins, asking the Lord again to forgive me, and joined the church. It was not a large church but was big on love; brother Ron Setser eventually took over the pastorate from his son who had pastored for a while. I was extremely active in my church in the choir doing solo work, teaching Sunday school out on visitation every Saturday, and loving the Lord and serving Him to the best of my ability.

* * *

In 1992, Ken called me telling me on a Friday afternoon in June we had stores in Georgia in trouble, and he needed me to move to Georgia because I was the only one who could fix them. I told him I had to pray about it and heard him draw in his breath and finally asked how long it would take to get an answer. I told him by Monday.

He offered me a $24,000 a year salary to make the move, and I wanted to be sure it was God moving me and not me because of the money as I was paying rent and the house payment at the same time. I asked the Lord for only two things: if He was moving me and I wasn't moving because of the money. The first thing was I would never have to drive on interstate 85 to get to work and secondly would have no money out of my own pocket to make the move. At that time, you made your move and then the company reimbursed you. I prayed all weekend seeking God's will and Monday, confident that God was moving me, called Ken to give him my answer. Brother Setser was floored when I told him what was going on because I was so active in my church and even working in the office to make sure the bulletins got out each service.

At that time, we had something called a shepherd's guide, which listed churches all over the country. I got it out searching for a church near the area. I was moving to and found Galilean Baptist Church in Norcross, Georgia. Pastor Setser wanted me to go to Shiloh Hills Baptist Church, but I told him I would have to go where the Lord wanted me to go Honestly Shiloh Hills is much farther away than I wanted to travel to go to church after I checked it out. I called Galilean speaking with Sue Lutz, the secretary, to ensure the standards were what they needed to be with Bible standards. All the answers were exactly what they needed to be, and I moved to Georgia the first week of July 1992, confident God wanted me to be at Galilean Baptist Church.

* * *

I left Florida with a $3,000 check in my pocket to pay my movers when I got to Georgia, and the company already had an apartment rented with first and last month's rent paid and the utilities turned on, and I have been in Georgia since 1992 and never had to drive on 85 to get to work. God is so good to me. Today, I continue to say I am more blessed than anyone I know of in this entire world. After opening two more stores in Georgia, I settled into the customer service manager position at our distribution center. Due to the expense of an apartment and a house payment. I called my brother in Ohio and talked to him, and my brothers decided to split the house payment with me to make it easier.

By 1997, the apartment I was living in decided to raise my rent $125, and I thought, *Lord, I can certainly buy something a lot cheaper than I can pay what they would charge me for the new rent.* I looked at the TV and saw a realtor there whom I called asking her where she went to church. She answered my question and then asked why, and I told her neither of us knew where I belonged but God knew, and if she didn't know and trust God, she couldn't find my new home. I told her the Lord let me know I could pay $60,000 for a condo to which she replied I would never find anything for that. I told her she didn't understand. Neither she nor I knew where it was, but God knew right where it was. The first she took me to was $70,000, the second place I currently live in today, and it was purchased for $59,900. God knew exactly what he was doing. I knew the moment I walked into the condo where I belonged.

I eventually wound up taking the customer service manager position at our distribution center. Ken Fletcher died at the Anderson Cancer Center in Texas on the operating table, and to the best of my knowledge, she never came to know the Lord.

In June 2000, our CEO called me from Ohio saying he understood I was having prayer meetings in my office. I told him I was, each morning we prayed for the business and each other. He told me he loved me but could not allow me to do that. I remember telling him, "Bob, if you take God's hand off of this business, we will lose it." The last four words he ever spoke to me were "I can't help it" in December 2000, the company took chapter 13.

When liquidators came in, I wasn't about to see thirty years of my life torn apart, took my three weeks' vacation, went home, laid my keys down on the coffee table, and told the Lord I never wanted to be in the furniture business again. I worked for a period of time in Covington with a computer company and one of our former Roberds employees called to ask if I was currently working. I had just resigned my job in Covington, and he said they needed someone to run customer service. In November 2000, God sent me to work for Mike Hall at then Plan It Oak at the warehouse close to my condo.

After thirty years of being with Ken Fletcher and him not wanting me to talk about the Lord, it was totally different at my new job. Truly this is where God wanted me. I started to work there the first part of November, and when we had our Thanksgiving dinner at the warehouse with the company providing the meat and us bringing side dishes, we were standing in the break room, and Mike looked at me and asked me to say the blessing. I did but I really thought I had died and gone to heaven that never would've happened at Roberds. I worked for Mike for eighteen years, and the entire time he let me be God's woman on the job.

Today on my mantle I have a sign that hung on the bulletin board in my office for everyone to see clearly. A day hemmed in prayer seldom unravels. Anyone could walk into my office that needed prayer, and I could pray with them not even having to close the door. Praise the Lord, and if Mike was in the warehouse, he'd come in and pray with us. It truly was a blessing!

After ten years of service, Mike presented every employee with a sapphire and diamond ring. When he presented mine to me, I couldn't help but I had tears in my eyes and today it makes me emotional. He said if we have a spiritual leader, it's Jerry. What a blessing to be with this man all those years. Tim Padden, our vice president, led many young people to the Lord and took many to church with him; there was no hiding the benefits of the Lord Jesus Christ in our business for which I will be eternally grateful that Tim and Mike allowed me to do what God wanted me to do. I am remembering a time that our bookkeeper came into my office all upset because she was in the process of getting a divorce. She was worried about things and under the glass on my desk I had a little card. I don't even remember where I got it from, but it was a little pink card and it said, "Worry slanders every promise God ever made," so I took it out from under my glass and gave it to Bee after I had held her while she cried and prayed for her.

I remember a conversation I had with one of our young ladies at the store Cani. She was all upset it was the anniversary of the date of her divorce. I told her I would meet her at the Cracker Barrel for lunch, and I took her to lunch while we were sitting there at that table by the window. I took my New Testament out, and she accepted the Lord Jesus Christ as her own personal Savior there in the Cracker Barrel restaurant. After lunch when we went into the parking lot, she said, "Now I've got something wonderful to remember, and today, I praise God for every one of our young people He allowed me to lead to Him while I worked there, and I will forever praise Mike and Tim again for allowing me to be God's woman on the job not having to hide my faith.

www.ingramcontent.com/pod-product-compliance
Lightning Source LLC
LaVergne TN
LVHW041553060526
838200LV00037B/1274